D1615876

This edition published 2020
by Ascension Publishing, LLC.

Originally published as
My First Picture Bible
by Anno Domini Publishing
(Hertfordshire, UK).

Copyright © 2013
Anno Domini Publishing
Text copyright © 2013 Jan Godfrey
Illustrations copyright © 2013 Angela Jolliffe

ISBN 978-1-950784-28-8

My Catholic
PICTURE BIBLE STORIES

JAN GODFREY and **ANGELA JOLLIFFE**

Time Period Name	Time Period Color	Book(s) of the Bible
Early World	Turquoise	Genesis 1-11
Patriarchs	Burgundy	Genesis 12-50
Egypt & Exodus	Red	Exodus
Desert Wanderings	Tan	Numbers
Conquest & Judges	Green	Joshua, Judges, 1 Samuel 1-8
Royal Kingdom	Purple	1 Samuel 9-31, 2 Samuel, 1 Kings 1-11
Divided Kingdom	Black	1 Kings 12-22, 2 Kings 1-16
Exile	Baby Blue	2 Kings 17-25
Return	Yellow	Ezra, Nehemiah
Maccabean Revolt	Orange	1 Maccabees
Messianic Fulfillment	Gold	Luke
The Church	White	Acts

All *Great Adventure Kids* books are color-coded to show where each story fits in Bible history.

This makes it easy to discover how the people and events of the Bible fit together to reveal the remarkable story of our Faith. For more information, visit **ascensionpress.com**.

Contents

God's wonderful world

Once upon a time, long, long ago, God made all the world. He made the light and the darkness, the sun, moon, and stars, the sky and the sea and everything in it.

God made the trees and the fields, the fruit and the flowers,

4

the mountains and rivers and creatures and birds.
And then he made people like you and like me to
look after his world and care for his world, his
beautiful, wonderful, marvelous world.

The great and terrible flood

God was sad because his people didn't love him. Only a man called Noah talked with God and listened when God talked to him.

"There's going to be a flood," said God to Noah. "So build a boat, a floating ark, to keep your family safe."

"OK," said Noah. When the ark was ready, it rained and it rained and it rained. But all Noah's family and all the animals, two by two by two, stayed safe in the ark, until the earth dried up and a rainbow shone out of a clear blue sky.

That rainbow was a sign of God's promise.

Noah thanked God for keeping his family and all the animals safe from the great and terrible flood.

Lots and lots of stars

One night, Abraham sat under the twinkling stars.

"Can you count the stars?" asked God. "One day you will have many, many children – more than all the stars in the sky."

Abraham was very puzzled. He had no children at all and he was getting old.

But one day he and his wife Sarah did have a little boy, called Isaac.

Much later... just as God had said, there were a great many families descended from Abraham living on the earth – more than all the stars in the sky!

A ladder of angels

Jacob, Isaac's son, had a quarrel with his twin brother, Esau. He was frightened, and he ran away.

He slept outside on the cold ground, with a stone for a pillow.

That night Jacob dreamed there were angels going up and down a shining stairway.

Then God himself spoke to Jacob.

"Don't be afraid," said God. "I will be with you wherever you go."

Jacob was so filled with wonder at hearing God's voice that he marked the place with a stone – the very stone that had been his pillow.

He called the place Bethel – God's house.

Joseph and his brothers

Jacob had a favorite son called Joseph. Joseph had strange dreams – that one day he would rule over all his family. So Joseph's brothers didn't like him at all... They made sure he went far away to live in Egypt.

One night the King of Egypt had strange dreams too.

"God is telling us to save lots of corn for when people are hungry," said Joseph. So Joseph was given the very important job of storing all the corn.

After a while, Joseph's brothers were very hungry. They came to Egypt to buy some corn. They didn't know who Joseph was – but Joseph knew who they were!

"Look, it's me!" said Joseph.

"But we thought you were dead," said his brothers in surprise. Then there were happy hugs all around.

"God was looking after me always and everywhere," Joseph said. "He even used my hard times to save so many people."

13

The princess and the baby

Once there was a baby boy called Moses.

"Ssh, don't cry, the King will hear you," whispered his mother. The King of Egypt didn't like baby boys. So Moses' mother was very afraid of all the King's men.

She laid him in a cozy basket among the reeds, behind the rushes, by the River Nile, while his big sister Miriam kept watch over him.

"Waaahhh!" cried baby Moses. The King didn't hear him and the King's men didn't hear him but... the princess, the King's own daughter, heard him.

"Ssh, don't cry," said the princess. "I'll look after you, tiny little baby. But I'll need someone to help me."

"I'll find someone to help," said big sister Miriam, and she ran to fetch her mother, baby Moses' mother!

God kept Moses safe from the King of Egypt, and his mother still took care of him.

16

The burning bush

First his mother took care of baby Moses, then the princess. But when he was a man, God took care of him.

One day, when Moses was looking after his sheep, he saw a bright and fiery bush – that didn't burn! God spoke to Moses out of the bush.

"Take off your shoes, Moses," said God. "This is a special, holy place."

Then God told Moses it was his turn to take care of other people.

"The king is being cruel to my people," said God. "I want you to lead them to another country where they will be safe."

"I can't do that!" said Moses. "It's much too hard for me."

"I'll help you," said God. "Take your brother Aaron with you, and you'll need your wooden stick."

Some horrible plagues

Moses and his brother Aaron went to see the King.

"God says, 'Let my people go,'" said Moses.

"No way," said the King. "Don't even think about it."

"There'll be trouble... ," said Moses. But the King wouldn't listen. And there was trouble.

The rivers and streams turned ugly and red.

"Let my people go," said Moses to the King – again and again and again.

"No!" said the King.

So there were frogs – everywhere, hopping into ovens and even into beds! There were clouds of buzzing gnats and flies, hailstones, and swarming insects that ate all the crops. The sky became dark for three whole days, and worst of all, lots of baby boys died.

"Enough! Just take your people and... GO AWAY!!" said the King.

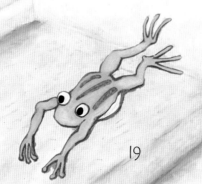

20

A road through the sea

Moses and the people left the King and his country. God showed them the way with a fiery cloud until they reached the big Red Sea. It looked impossible to cross.

"The King is chasing us!" they said. "But the sea is in front of us!"

Moses held up the special wooden stick, and a strong wind began to blow a path through the high, watery waves. Moses and his people marched all night across the sea bed, and by morning they reached the other side, safe and dry.

"Now hold your stick over the sea," God said to Moses. The waters ran together and flowed back again – and all the King's men were left behind them.

How to be happy

High on a smoky, thundery mountain, God spoke to Moses. As Moses climbed, there was a trumpet blast and the terrified people stayed down below. When Moses reached the top of the mountain, he listened carefully.

"You must worship me and no one else," said God. "You must love me and other people with all your heart. You must not hurt or kill, or steal or tell lies and say bad things. You must love your family and be happy with the things you have.

"Do all this and you will be happy."

Down came the walls!

The land God had promised his people was not far away. But there was a city of fierce men surrounded by big, high walls in front of them.

God's people looked up at the people of Jericho.

The people of Jericho looked down at them.

"We'll never get into Jericho," wailed God's people.

"God will help us," said Joshua.

Joshua sent some of his soldiers to march around and around the city walls. Others blew their trumpets VERY VERY LOUDLY!!

Then down came the walls!

Gideon's fleece

"Gideon!" said an angel. "God wants you to help his people."

"Me? Are you sure you mean me?" said Gideon. "Will you help me to be really, really sure?"

That night Gideon put out a woolly fleece. Would it be wet and dewy in the morning while the ground was dry? It was!

But Gideon still wasn't sure.

So the next night, he put out a woolly fleece again. Would it be dry in the morning while the ground was wet and dewy? It was!

Now Gideon was really sure that God had spoken to him.

God speaks to Samuel

"Please, God, help me," Hannah prayed. "I want to have a baby SO much."

Hannah was VERY happy when *baby Samuel* was born.

When he was older, Hannah took him to the temple where he could grow up to love God like the kind, wise old priest called Eli.

One night, Samuel heard someone calling his name: once, twice, three times he heard it.

"Samuel!"

He thought it was Eli, but it wasn't.

"Go back to bed," said Eli each time.

But Samuel heard his name again.

Then the kind, wise old priest, Eli, knew that God was speaking to Samuel. He told Samuel to listen carefully.

"I am listening, God," said Samuel.

"I will always listen to you."

God chooses David

Jesse's sons stood in front of Samuel. One, two, three, four, five, six, seven.

God had asked Samuel to choose the next King.

"Don't just choose the tallest or the strongest," whispered God to Samuel. "Choose the one who's good and wise and true."

"Do you have another son?" Samuel asked Jesse.

Jesse's youngest son, David, was looking after the sheep.

As Samuel looked at David, God told him that David was good and wise and true.

"You will be the next King," said Samuel, and poured special oil on David's head. David loved God. He knew that God would always help him.

David and Goliath

Everyone was afraid of Goliath. He was a big, bad, fierce GIANT of a bully! King Saul was afraid and his soldiers were afraid.

"I'll fight him," said David. "God has helped me fight lions and bears. I'm not afraid."

"WHOOOO are YOOOOU?" roared the giant, towering above David.

"Just you wait and see," said David, and he took five pebbles from the stream. He aimed one of the pebbles at Goliath using his shepherd's sling, and kerplunk! That was the end of the big, bad, fierce giant – and all because David trusted God to help him.

Elijah and the ravens

"It's not going to rain for a long time," said God to his friend Elijah. "Go and tell the king that it is his fault."

So Elijah told the king, who wasn't happy to hear that.

"Go and hide from the king beside a little stream, way over there," God told Elijah. "You'll have enough to drink, and big birds called ravens will bring you food."

So Elijah drank from the little stream, and ravens brought him food every day, just as God had said. When the little stream became a trickle and then dried up because there still hadn't been any rain, God told Elijah it was time to go.

Enough flour, enough oil

"I will show you where to go next," God told Elijah.

Elijah met a poor woman gathering sticks to light a little fire.

"Bake me some bread," said Elijah. "Please?"

"But I don't have enough flour and I don't have enough oil," said the woman. "This is the last meal my son and I will ever eat!"

"Trust God," said Elijah. "He has promised that you'll have enough until it rains again."

So the woman baked Elijah some bread, and when she looked, there was enough flour and enough oil to bake bread for them all another day. God gave them enough to eat until the day it rained again.

Choose God!

It hadn't rained for three years and King Ahab was angry with Elijah.

"Let's see who'll send fire and rain," said Elijah. "Will it be the true and living God, or your Baal who is made of stone?"

Everyone laid out wood and stones for cooking.

"Baal! Baal!" shouted the people, and they danced about and waved their arms. Nothing happened.

"Maybe Baal is playing hide-and-seek," teased Elijah. Then he prayed to God.

"You are the one true God," said Elijah. "Please, send down fire!"

And suddenly there were fiery flames and sizzling smoke... and everyone wanted to worship the true and living God.

A little while later, God sent rain once more to water the earth.

Jonah and the big fish

God told Jonah to go to Nineveh, a city where the people did lots of bad things.

Jonah didn't want to go. Instead he got on a ship and sailed away. A big storm frightened everyone on the ship. Jonah knew God wanted him to go back.

"Throw me into the sea!" Jonah said.

As he fell into the water, God sent a very

big fish to swallow him. For three days Jonah stayed in the fish's dark tummy. Then the big fish threw Jonah out on to the beach.

Wooosh!

This time Jonah went to Nineveh. He told the people they needed to say sorry to God and then do good things...

God forgives

The people of Nineveh listened. They were sorry for the wrong things they'd done.

"We've been bad," they said.

"We've been cruel and unkind. We're really, truly sorry."

God was pleased that the people were sorry. God was happy to forgive them.

But Jonah wasn't happy. Jonah was very grumpy. Jonah sat under a vine and sulked.

"I knew you'd be kind and loving and forgiving," said Jonah. "But I think those people deserve to be punished!"

But God is kind and loving and forgiving. He was happy that the people were sorry. God was happy that they stopped doing bad things.

Daniel and the lions

Daniel loved God and worshipped him.

He prayed to him every day beside his open window.

"Daniel shouldn't pray to God," said the king's men. "Daniel should pray to the king!"

So Daniel was thrown into the lions' den.

The king liked Daniel. He didn't want him to die. The king was so worried that he couldn't sleep.

Early the next day he went to the lions' den.

"Good morning," said Daniel, to the king's great surprise. "God has taken good care of me."

Daniel was still alive! The lions were quietly walking around.

"That's amazing!" said the king. "Your God can save people. Your God is GREAT! Everyone should worship him."

45

Mary and Joseph

God had promised that one day a very special child would be born who would share God's mercy and love with the world in a new way. This is what happened...

An angel came to tell Mary that she would be the mother of God's Son. Mary could hardly believe that God had chosen her.

Mary had to travel with her husband Joseph to Bethlehem so the Romans could count everyone. But there was no room for them to stay. So Mary's baby, Jesus, God's Son, had his first bed in the manger where the animals ate their hay.

Angels in the sky

On the night that Jesus was born,
shepherds were out on the cold, dark hills with
their sheep. They were very sleepy...

Then... suddenly they were very much awake!

The sky was full of bright, beautiful light, and they heard
angels singing heavenly music.

"Glory to God!" sang the angels. "God's Son has been born! Go to Bethlehem and you will find him lying in a manger."

When the angels had gone, the shepherds ran to Bethlehem and found the baby Jesus just as the angels said – lying in a manger.

They sang praises to God that night. They had seen God's Son, the baby born to change the world.

Following the star

High in the sky, a very bright star shone out into the darkness.

"This is a sign from God!" said some wise and clever men. "A new king has been born! We must take him gifts and worship him."

It was a long journey, but the travelers followed the star all the way.

When the star came to rest over a little house, the wise men found Mary, Joseph, and the baby Jesus.

"We have brought gifts," said the wise men, kneeling down in great wonder to worship God's Son. "We have brought gold, frankincense, and myrrh."

Catching fish

Jesus was a man now. He was sitting in his friend Peter's boat. "Put your boats further out to sea," said Jesus to his friends. "Then you'll catch some fish."

"We've worked hard all night, and we haven't caught anything!" said Peter. "But OK – if you say so."

They let down their nets into the deep sea, and suddenly the nets were so full of fish that they nearly broke, and the boats were so full of fish that they nearly sank. There were fish everywhere!

"Follow me," said Jesus, "and tell everyone all about God. It will be just like catching fish!"

Four good friends

A man lay ill on a mat. His friends wanted to help him. They knew that Jesus could heal people. They hoped Jesus would heal their friend.

"We'll never get through!" they said when they saw all the people crowded in a house talking to Jesus.

Then they had a good idea. They climbed the steps up to the roof of the house and started to make a big hole! Then they carefully let the mat down. The man and the mat landed right at Jesus' feet!

"Pick up your mat and go home," Jesus said kindly. "Your sins are forgiven." The man found that he could get up. He could walk! He could carry his mat home! Jesus had healed their friend, inside and out!

His friends were VERY happy!

Truly happy

Jesus and his friends sat together high on a grassy hillside. The people all listened carefully as Jesus told them what God was like and how they could be truly happy.

"Be kind and loving and patient," said Jesus.

"Then you'll be happy. Be helpful and generous and truthful. Then you'll be happy. Don't quarrel or say nasty things about each other. Then you'll be happy."

"Follow God and love him, and you'll be like tiny tasty grains of salt or bright little lights all over the world. And you'll be truly happy!"

Wind and waves

Jesus and his friends were in a boat out on a big lake. It was very calm and quiet and still, and Jesus fell asleep.

Suddenly a storm blew up. The wind blew hard, and big waves rocked and tossed the boat.

"WAKE UP!" shouted Jesus' friends, who were very frightened. Jesus stood up.

"Ssh, be quiet," he called out to the wind and the waves.

Then... the wind and the waves died down, and everywhere was calm and quiet and still again.

The storm had gone away.

His friends were amazed. "Jesus can even calm a storm," they said.

Bread and fish

One evening, everyone was hungry. They had been following Jesus and listening to him all day.

"It's late, and there's nothing to eat!" said Jesus' friends, looking at the huge crowd of people.

Then a little boy shared his picnic. He had five pieces of bread and two small fish.

"Thank you," Jesus said to the boy. "Thank you!" said Jesus to God, and they shared the food that Jesus had blessed.

And then, by a miracle, everyone in that enormous crowd had enough to eat! They had a very happy time together – and there were even twelve baskets of food left over!

The lost sheep

Jesus was telling a story.

"Once upon a time there was a shepherd who had a hundred sheep. One little sheep wandered off one day. It strayed up into the hills where it was soon lost and cold and frightened.

"'Baa!' said the little sheep sadly.

"The shepherd still had ninety-nine sheep safe and sound, but... he couldn't stop thinking about the little sheep, lost and cold and frightened.

"The shepherd went looking for his lost sheep. He wasn't happy until he had found it and was carrying it home on his shoulder.

"'Look how happy I am!' said the shepherd to everyone. 'I've found my lost sheep!'

"God loves you as the shepherd loves his sheep. He'll always come looking for you when you are lost," said Jesus.

63

The good Samaritan

Jesus was telling another story.

"Once a man was badly hurt by some thieves. They took his clothes and his money and left him by the side of the road.

"An important person came by.

"'Oh dear,' said the important person, but he walked away quickly on the other side of the road.

"Another important person came by.

"'Oh dear,' he said. 'Robbers!' He walked away quickly too.

"Then another man came along. He was a stranger from another country, but he stopped to help. He bathed the injured man's wounds and took him on his donkey to a nearby inn.

"Who do you think did the right thing that day?" asked Jesus.

The man who shouted

A man called Bartimaeus had eyes that couldn't see anything at all – no flowers or trees or sunshine or people. But the same man could hear very well – and one day he heard that Jesus was coming along the road.

"Help me, Jesus!" called the man.

"Sshh," said everyone grumpily.

So Bartimaeus tried again.

"Jesus – HELP ME!!" he shouted, really loudly.

"Bring that man to me," said Jesus.

"Please – I want to see!" said Bartimaeus.

Jesus smiled.

"Go on your way – you can see," he said.

Then Bartimaeus could see again – the flowers and the trees and the sunshine and the people – and Jesus himself!

68

Zacchaeus climbs a tree

Zacchaeus was very small and he was very rich but he didn't have many friends. That's because Zacchaeus was a cheat.

When Jesus came along the road one day, Zacchaeus wanted to see him very much. But Zacchaeus was very small and everyone else was very tall...

So Zacchaeus climbed up into a tree with low spreading branches and looked down at everyone below.

Then he saw Jesus!

"Come down," said Jesus, smiling. "I'm coming to your house today."

At home, Zacchaeus told Jesus he was sorry for the wrong things he'd done.

"I'll give everyone back their money and share the rest with anyone who needs it," he said.

Then Zacchaeus and Jesus – and everyone else! – were very happy.

Jesus rides a donkey

One day, Jesus rode into Jerusalem on a donkey.
    Crowds of people followed him to the big
city of Jerusalem: men and women and lots of
children. It was noisy! It was exciting!
    They threw down their cloaks in front of the
donkey. They threw down palm branches and
waved them in the air. They shouted and cheered!
        "Hosanna!" they shouted.
        "God is great!"
        "Praise King Jesus!"

71

A very bad secret

Judas was greedy and he did something very, very bad. He went secretly to see Jesus' enemies. They whispered and plotted bad things together.

"I'll take your soldiers to find Jesus when it's dark," said Judas. "But... what will you pay me?"

"Thirty silver coins," said Jesus' enemies. They counted them out – ten... twenty... thirty.

Then greedy Judas went to find Jesus, feeling the coins in his pocket.

An important meal

The Passover was a special meal of wine with bread and lamb and herbs. It was a happy time. But Jesus knew this would be the last meal he would eat with his friends.

"One of you here tonight has decided not to be my friend anymore," Jesus said sadly. "One of you has made friends with my enemies."

"Not me?" they said.

"No, not me!" Peter said.

"And not me," Judas said, looking at his feet.

"Remember me," said Jesus. He broke some bread, blessed it, and shared it. "This is my body." He blessed a cup of wine and shared it. "This is my blood."

Then Jesus took his friends out into the dark night, to a garden full of olive trees. And Jesus asked God to help him.

Peter is afraid

Judas came with soldiers that night. The soldiers arrested Jesus. Jesus watched his friends run away.

But Peter followed. He waited outside in the darkness while Jesus was asked lots of questions.

"Aren't you his friend?" a girl asked Peter.

"No!" said Peter, very afraid.

"Yes, you are his friend," said another.

"No, no!" said Peter again.

"You are, aren't you?" they said, coming closer.

"No, no! NO!" said Peter.

Then the early morning cockerel crowed. What had Peter done? He felt so ashamed, he cried.

77

78

A crown of thorns

Pontius Pilate was an important man. He must choose: Should Jesus go free? Should he be killed?

He stood in front of a big crowd of people.

"What do you want me to do with Jesus?" Pilate asked them.

"Crucify him!" shouted the people. "Crucify him!"

The people who had paid Judas had also paid people in the crowd. Pilate gave Jesus to his soldiers.

They teased Jesus. They put a crown of sharp thorns on his head.

"Long live the King!" they laughed.

The saddest day ever

Then Jesus' enemies put him to death on a cross between two thieves.

The soldiers laughed and played games with dice.

Jesus asked God to forgive everyone in the whole world for all the bad and unkind things that anyone had ever done.

Jesus' mother, Mary, was there. She felt very, very sad.

"My friend John will look after you," said Jesus quietly.

Then there was a rumbling earthquake. The sun went in and the sky turned dark, even though it was the middle of the day.

Then Jesus died. It was the saddest day there had ever been.

A very quiet garden

Later that day, a rich man called Joseph, who had been a friend of Jesus, carried Jesus' body to his own quiet and beautiful garden.

Joseph had spoken bravely to Pilate himself.

"Yes, now he is dead, you may take Jesus away to bury him," said Pilate to Joseph.

Another friend of Jesus, Nicodemus, helped Joseph. The two friends gently laid Jesus in a cool, dark, rocky cave and pushed a very big and heavy stone across the doorway. Nobody could possibly get in or out now.

Jesus' mother, Mary, and some other friends came to the quiet garden too.

They were very, very sad.

83

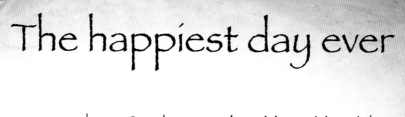

The happiest day ever

Then... very early on Sunday morning, Mary Magdalene and her friends went to the place where Jesus was buried.

But the big and heavy stone had been rolled away!

Two angels shone beside the cave.

"Jesus has risen from the dead!" said the angels.

Some of the women ran to tell Peter and John.

But Mary Magdalene stayed behind, weeping by the empty tomb.

"Why are you crying?" said a voice behind her.

Mary realized she was talking to... Jesus!

"You are alive!" she shouted as the birds sang on that very first Easter day.

Jesus meets Thomas

Thomas had *been* one of Jesus' friends. He just couldn't believe that Jesus was alive again.

"I need to *see* his hands and feet," said Thomas.

"But Jesus is alive!" said his friends. "Really, truly alive! We have *seen* him!"

"But I need to *see* him too. I need to touch the places where the soldiers hurt him," said Thomas.

A few days later Jesus suddenly appeared in a room where all his friends were together. This time, Thomas was there too.

"Peace be with you," smiled Jesus.

Then Jesus spoke to Thomas.

"Look at me, Thomas. Touch my wounds for yourself."

"It really IS you!" said Thomas in wonder. "You are my Lord and my God!"

Breakfast on the beach

Peter and his friends went fishing one night, out on Lake Galilee – but they couldn't catch any fish at all. They felt tired and disappointed and grumpy.

"Try again!" called a voice from the water's edge.

This time they caught a huge number of wriggling fish. They could hardly pull in the net!

"It's Jesus!" said the friends.

"Come and eat," said Jesus as they dragged in the fish.

Jesus had made a little fire, and they all had breakfast of fish and bread. It tasted good!

Then Jesus said to Peter, "I want you to do something special for me, Peter. Love me and follow me, and take care of all my friends."

Then Peter knew that Jesus had forgiven him for saying he didn't know him at all.

Back to heaven

Jesus appeared to many of his friends after he rose from the dead. He told his friends that they would take the Good News to the whole world, and baptize in the name of the Father, the Son, and the Holy Spirit.

Then one day, Jesus stood with his friends on a high hill. "Will you be our real King one day?" they asked Jesus.

"One day," said Jesus. "But first I'm going back to my Father God in heaven. I will always be there to help you."

As he spoke, a cloud covered him, and Jesus went back up to heaven.

The friends gazed up at the empty sky.

Two angels stood there with them.

"Why are you looking up at the sky?" said the angels. "Jesus has gone; but he will come back again one day."

Wind and fire

Jesus' friends were all together for a special feast called Pentecost. They were afraid that they would be hurt as Jesus had been. Suddenly there was a noisy, rushing wind blowing through the whole room.

There were bright little flames everywhere that danced about and touched everyone.

Then Jesus' friends realized that they could speak in other languages, and they weren't afraid anymore either!

Peter - the same Peter who had told people he didn't know Jesus at all - stood up and explained that God's Spirit had come to help him... and everyone who loved Jesus.

"Jesus is God's Son," said Peter. "He came to earth to die for us. He's alive again, and he will forgive everything anyone has done wrong. And his Spirit will help us live the way he wants us to."

Sharing and caring

Crowds of people listened to Peter and believed in God. They became friends of Jesus too, and they asked God's Spirit to help them.

People who were afraid or selfish became brave and loving and kind. They were able to heal people who were ill. They helped people who were sad and lonely.

"We'll sell our houses to help other people," they said.

"We'll share all our money and our things," they said.

"We'll share all our food," they said.

They prayed and praised God together. They ate meals together happily. They met together in the temple to learn more about God. They remembered Jesus' words at the Last Supper, and shared his Body and Blood.

Every day more and more people chose to love God and were baptized. They all praised and thanked him for making them so happy.

95

The man at the gate

*O*ne day Peter and John went to pray at the temple.

There was a man sitting by the gate there who'd never been able to walk. He begged people for money every day as they went into the temple.

"Please," said the poor, lame man, staring hopefully at Peter and John. "Please... please..."

Peter stopped to talk to him.

"I don't have any money," said Peter. "But I can give you something better. Jesus has healed you – get up: you can walk!"

Straightaway the man got up and he didn't just walk – he ran and jumped and praised God!

Everyone at the temple could hardly believe their eyes, because the man who couldn't walk was... walking!

In and out of prison

King Herod didn't like Peter and his friends. He didn't like them talking about God and about Jesus.

So he put Peter in prison and chained him up.

"We must ask God to help Peter," said his friends.

That night, an angel appeared in the prison while Peter was asleep.

"Wake up, Peter!" said the angel. "Get up and follow me!"

The chains fell away as Peter followed the angel. Heavy iron gates opened for him. The guards didn't notice him. Peter was free!

Peter went to find his friends. He had to hammer really hard at the door.

Knock! Knock! Knock!

"Look, it's Peter!" said his friends. "God has answered our prayers!"

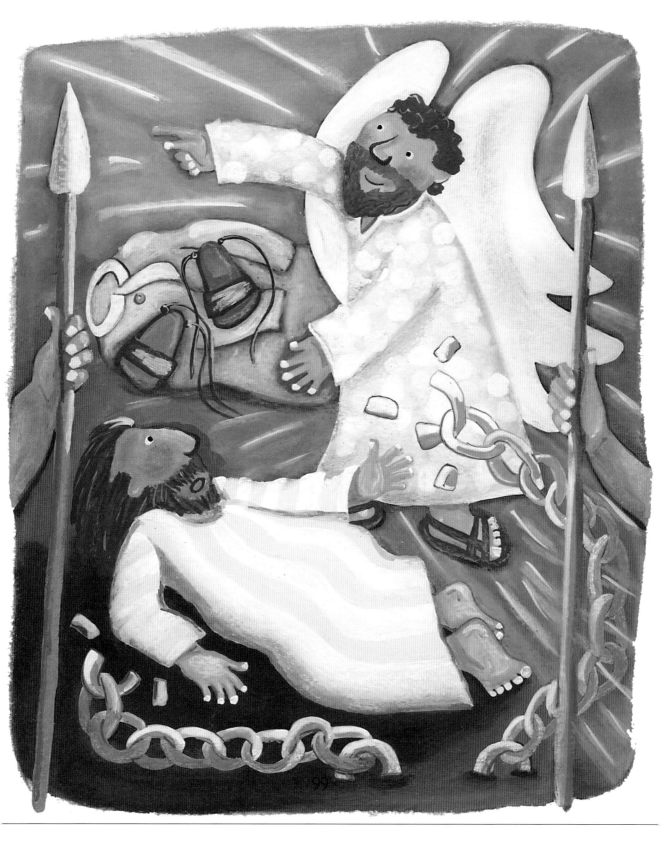

All God's creatures

Later on, Peter stayed at a house by the sea that belonged to a friend called Simon.

One day, Peter was resting in the sunshine up on the flat roof of Simon's house. He was hungry, but lunch wasn't quite ready, and he fell asleep.

Peter dreamed about a big sheet of creatures of all shapes and sizes. Then Peter heard God's voice.

"You can eat any kind of food that you choose, Peter," said God.

"But some of these creatures are bad to eat," said Peter.

"It's all right, Peter," said God. "All of these are now good to eat."

When Peter woke up, he found that God had sent three men to see him.

"Go with them," said God.

All God's children

Cornelius was a good man who was also a Roman soldier. He and his family often prayed to God. An angel had told Cornelius to send the three visitors to Peter.

"Go and find Peter, who's staying at Simon's house beside the sea," the angel had said. So Cornelius sent the three men to Simon's house right away.

When Peter reached Cornelius' house, there was a room filled with all sorts of people. They were as different from each other as the creatures in Peter's dream.

Then Peter understood that God was using the dream to tell him something very important.

"God loves everyone, whoever they are and wherever they live, and whatever they eat and drink," said Peter.

"Praise God!" said all the people in all sorts of different languages. "Praise God! He loves ALL of us!"

A good man called Stephen

Stephen was one of Jesus' friends. When people were poor and hungry, Stephen helped them with food and money.

But some people didn't like Stephen because he loved Jesus. They pretended he'd done bad things.

Stephen looked at his enemies and listened to them as they said bad things about him. He was not angry.

"His face looks true and good and full of light, like an angel," someone said.

Then Stephen's enemies became very angry.

They shouted at him. They dragged him away. They threw stones and rocks at him.

"Dear God – forgive my enemies for doing this," prayed Stephen with his dying breath.

A young man called Saul was looking and listening and watching.

"Good," said Saul, who hated all Jesus' friends at that time. "YES! I'm glad Stephen was punished."

105

A big surprise for Saul

Angry Saul set off for the city of Damascus. He wanted all Jesus' friends to be put in prison or killed.

Suddenly a great light streamed all around Saul, and he heard a voice speaking his name. He fell to the ground.

"Saul! Saul! Why do you want to hurt me? Why do you want to hurt my friends?" Then Saul understood that this was the voice of Jesus.

"What do you want me to do?" asked Saul.

"Go into the city," said the voice. "I will send someone to help you."

Saul tried to get to his feet, but the great light had blinded him. His friends had to lead him by the hand into Damascus.

After three days Saul could see again. And now, instead of being one of Jesus' enemies, Saul was one of Jesus' best friends!

Saul becomes Paul

When Saul became a friend of Jesus, he became a much nicer person. He loved other people instead of hating them. He wanted to help them instead of hurting them. He even changed his name – from Saul... to Paul!

Paul had a very exciting time telling people about Jesus.

But sometimes people grew really angry and didn't like what he said.

"God says you must not worship statues or do bad magic!" said Paul.

"God is the only true and living God. He can help you if you ask him – but don't worship things that are made with human hands."

Paul was sometimes chased away or beaten or put in prison. But nothing would stop him from telling people about God.

Gods and garlands

Paul went to all sorts of places, sometimes sailing over the sea, to tell people all about Jesus.

One day Paul traveled with Barnabas to a place called Lystra, where God healed a man who couldn't walk.

"Stand up!" said Paul, and soon the

man was walking again. All the people there got very excited and thought Paul and Barnabas were gods themselves.

"The gods have come!" they shouted. Suddenly there was a big procession with garlands of flowers and even a special bull to be killed.

"No! Stop!" shouted Paul and Barnabas to the crowds. "We're not gods! We're ordinary people. All we want to do is to tell you about the one true and living God!"

Prison praise

Later on, Paul and his friend Silas went to a town called Philippi.

When they went down to the river to pray, they met some women there. One, who was called Lydia, sold purple cloth. After she had listened to Paul speak about Jesus, she asked to be baptized as a Christian.

Paul and Silas stayed at her house for a while. But a little while later, they were chained up in prison.

At midnight they were singing praises to God when there was a very big earthquake. Their chains fell off and they were free! But no one tried to escape. Instead they helped the jailer by telling him about Jesus.

Not only had Lydia become a Christian, but now the jailer and his family were also baptized as Christians.

A rough sea journey

Paul and his friends made a long sea trip toward Rome. At first the sea was calm, but then a strong winter wind blew, harder and harder. The sailing ship was tossed about in the rough, heavy seas.

"We're lost!" cried the terrified sailors. "We're going to drown!"

"Don't worry," said Paul. "God has promised we shall all be safe!"

Next morning, near land, the ship hit a big sandbank and began to break up. Some people swam to the shore. Others grabbed pieces of wood from the ship and floated to the beach. But everyone was safe, just as God had promised!

Safe on the shore

God had brought Paul and all the sailors safely to the island called Malta.

"It's cold and wet and rainy!" they said. "But we are safe."

They were glad to be alive, and the island people were friendly and kind. They lit a warm fire for them.

Then a snake slithered out of the firewood. People were frightened when they saw that it was hanging from Paul's arm! But the snake didn't hurt Paul. He shook it off, and the people listened to what he said – they thought he must be very special if he was not hurt by the snake.

Paul was able to heal many people on the island while they were there, and he told them how much God wanted them to be God's friends.

Love from Paul

When Paul finally reached Rome, he wrote lots of letters to Jesus' friends. They lived in many different towns and cities.

Paul wrote them with a pen made from feathers or reeds, using thick and sticky ink on special paper called papyrus.

Paul thanked people who had been his friends, and encouraged them to tell other people about Jesus.

"Be faithful and true to God," wrote Paul. "Love God, care and share and forgive."

"Don't be afraid and don't worry," wrote Paul. "Pray to God, and he will help you. Shine out like lights in the world, and live as God wants you to, looking after each other.

"Whatever you do, the most important thing is to love each other – just as God loves you."

A holy, heavenly city

John was one of Jesus' friends. When he grew old, he lived on an island called Patmos, in the middle of a warm blue sea.

John loved God and worshipped him. He also wrote to some of Jesus' friends.

"God is very holy," wrote John. "He is the Lord God Almighty."

Then God showed John angels praising God and Jesus. God showed him a beautiful city sparkling like a jewel in the sunshine, with crystal rivers and beautiful leafy trees and streets that shone like golden glass. In God's new, holy, heavenly city there would be no sadness or hurting or crying, because God himself would live there and wipe away all the tears.

"I will come again soon," promised Jesus.

"Yes, Lord Jesus!" said John. "Come to be with everyone – please come soon."